© 2012 Arqueonautas Worldwide SA

"Spanish Coins in Mozambican Waters: The Numismatic Collection of the *São José* (1622)" by Alejandro Mirabal.

PHOTOS BY Anya Bartels-Suermont and Alejandro Mirabal.

TEXT REVISION BY Janette Ramsay.

EDITED BY Miguel Gomes da Costa.

EDITORIAL COORDINATION BY Nikolaus Graf Sandizell.

PUBLISHED BY Arqueonautas Worldwide - Arqueologia Subaquática SA, Rua das Murças, 98, 9000-058 Funchal. Portugal. All rights reserved.

www.aww.pt

ISBN: 978-989-97948-0-1

Contents

Preface 5

Acknowledgements 7

SECTION 1
Abstract 8

SECTION 2
Introduction 9

SECTION 3
The last voyage of the *São José* 10

SECTION 4
The wreck site and excavation of the coins 12

SECTION 5
The coins 24

MEXICAN COINS 25
SPANISH COIN 29
PERUVIAN COINS 31

SECTION 6
Metallurgic analysis applied 35

SECTION 7
The cargo of the São José 36

SECTION 8
Conclusions 41

SECTION 9
Bibliography and sources 44

Preface

Since the foundation of Arqueonautas in 1995, one of our objectives has been to put together a collection of our marine archaeology publications, in book form, to cover the major projects undertaken by our Company. Years have gone by without us being able to accomplish this goal as publishing books in a conventional is simply too expensive and therefore the on-line version of our scientific publications at **www.aww.pt** has had to suffice. Nevertheless, our determination to publish our own books has never waned and we are now, thanks to print-on-demand and ebooks, in a position to fulfil this long-standing ambition, for the first time.

We strongly believe that the quality and consistency of the archaeological work developed by Arqueonautas' archaeologists, experts and operations team, fully justifies publication in book form. Not only will these books do justice to the exemplary archaeological expeditions promoted by Arqueonautas in three different continents, but also allows for a wider dissemination of the scientific knowledge generated.

As such, with "Spanish Coins in Mozambican Waters: The Numismatic Collection of the São José (1622)" written by our Chief Archaeologist, Alejandro Mirabal, we are thrilled to initiate a new chapter in the ever evolving lifeline of Arqueonautas Worldwide.

Our commitment to protect and save World Maritime Heritage is further enhanced through this initiative, offering scholars, researchers and the general public, access to scientific studies of important historical wreck sites. This is of particular importance at a time when looting, net-trawling, coastal construction and the off-shore industries are responsible for a constant destruction of Underwater Cultural Heritage and the irrevocable loss that it represents to mankind.

In face of such demanding challenges, Arqueonautas stands for a pro-active marine archaeology policy, embodied here in the form of these publications that will promote a better understanding of the discovery and documentation of these unique time capsules lying on the seabed of the world's oceans.

We sincerely hope that our effort can contribute to a renewed interest in marine archaeology and raise awareness of the need to protect, save and study the remaining historical shipwreck sites, reflecting our deep felt passion and Arqueonautas' sole reason of existence.

Estoril, October 2012

Nikolaus Graf Sandizell
(Chairman of the Board & CEO of Arqueonautas Worldwide SA)

Acknowledgements

Like any academic research, "Spanish Coins in Mozambican waters: The Numismatic Collection of the *São José* (1622)" is the result of the combined effort of a large group of specialists. In this particular case the study was preceded by a complex field operation in a remote spot of the Mozambican geography, making this group even larger and more heterogeneous. Although without their hard work this publication wouldn't exist, mentioning them all would be impossible.

First I want to deeply thank Dr. Margaret Rule for her wise and continuous guidance and advise during these, by now, many years. To the numismatists Alfredo Días Gamez, Jorge A. Proctor, António Trigueiros and Carol Tedesco for their invaluable help in understanding the intricate world of the early 17th century coinage. To Alina Reyes for her zeal and meticulous recording of every single coin of the many thousands involved in this study, providing most of the data in which the research was based.

To the Ministério de Educação e Cultura of the Republic of Mozambique, for their support to the project.

To Dr. Jacinto Veloso from Património Internacional SARL and Urgel Barreira for providing us with liaison and logistics support from Maputo, Mozambique. To Nikolaus Sandizell, CEO of Arqueonautas Worldwide, for sponsoring this publication and supporting operations from Europe.

Finally I want to specially thank the Arqueonautas Team of Archaeologists, Archaeological divers, Skippers, Conservators, draftsman, IT specialists, deckhands and boatmen, lead by Operations Manager Eng. Faure Cambiella, who faced so many hardships and adverse weather during the excavation phase without lowering, even for one instant, the quality of the collected data.

Any achievement that this publication may contain is owed to all of them; the errors, that may plague it, are entirely mine.

M.Sc. Alejandro Mirabal Jorge
Marine Archaeologist

Abstract

The shipwreck codenamed MOG-003 was found in *Infusse* reef, *Mogincual*, in the Province of Nampula, Republic of Mozambique, in 2004 during a magnetometer survey of the area. It has been tentatively identified as the *São José*, a Portuguese Indiaman vice-flagship (*Almiranta*) from the 1622 fleet en route from Lisbon to Goa, India, lost at this location on the 24th of July of 1622 during a battle against the Anglo-Dutch fleet. The archaeological excavation of this wreck provided a collection of artefacts from the late 16th and the early 17th centuries which allowed the study of the numismatic and artillery aspects of that time. The evidence confirms that the *São José* was carrying Spanish *reales* minted in the Americas and Spain, belonging to the Portuguese crown.

Key words: MOG-003, *São José*, Mozambique, 1622 fleet, Spanish *reales, cruzados*.

Introduction

At the end of the 16th and beginning of the 17th centuries in Europe, international trade with the Far East followed either the secular route of the Mediterranean and the Red Sea through the Turkish empire, which functioned as intermediary, or along the maritime route of the Cape of Good Hope, discovered and explored by the Portuguese sailors since 1498-1499.

During the first half of the 16th century, the cargoes of spices from the naus returning to Portugal were paid above all with European merchandise (predominantly copper and German silver) and with the gold brought from the Portuguese mines in West Africa and coined in Lisbon. During the second half of the century, this practice changed and gold was practically replaced with silver, which was no longer of European but rather of American origin, from the West Indies of Castile.

Today we know that the amounts of American silver imported during the 16th and 17th centuries, which entered through the port of Seville, were 44 tons on average per year between 1521 and 1580 and 270 tons on average per year, between 1591 and 1600, when a production peak was reached. During the second half of the 16th century in Europe, German silver mines were not able to produce more than 20 tons per year (*Vilar*, 1990, p.197). This abundance of American silver led to the foundation of new mint houses in Peru: in Lima in 1565 and in Potosi in 1573. Together with the mint house of Mexico which had been founded in 1537, they would go on to mint a coin of universal circulation for the whole century to come: the 8 *reales* coin (*real de a ocho*), worth 8 single *reales*, or 272 *maravedis* of copper, later also known as peso fuerte or peso duro, which would set the future model for the Turkish *piastra* and the North-American Dollar.

Simultaneous to the influx of Spanish *reales* minted in the Americas at the end of the 16th and beginning of the 17th centuries, Europe started developing a taste for other oriental products such as silks, porcelains and tea, merchandise which resulted from the large scale development of the Portuguese trade with the Chinese world through Macau, always paid for with silver.

The Portuguese were well acquainted with the ins and outs of the Far Eastern trade, from the coasts of Malabar to Malacca and following up to the far away coasts of China and Japan. The Portuguese were the first to try to introduce the Castilian *reales* to the trade route with the Far East, which they achieved by diverging the course of the American silver to the ports of the Azores and Lisbon (*Trigueiros*, 2009, no *prelo*).

At the end of the 16th and beginning of the 17th centuries, when Portugal was politically but not economically united to Spain, the *naus* that left Lisbon towards Cochin, Goa, Malacca and Macau transported specie predominantly in the form of Spanish *reales*, as was later the case with their maritime competitors. The Portuguese lost the monopoly of the maritime trade of eastern spices during the first years of the 1600s, due to the infiltration of the English and Dutch Companies of East India. They were thus forced to export silver in the form of *reales* from Castile to buy the desired spices, as their native merchandise was of no use on the stops along the trade routes.

The last voyage of the *São José*

On the 18th of March 1622, the Portuguese fleet left Lisbon on their annual trip to Goa, India. That year the convoy carried, besides the usual trade money, a very important nobleman: Dom Francisco da Gama, fourth Count of Vidigueira, who had been recently appointed 22nd Viceroy of India. The fleet was led by flagship (*Capitânia*) *Santa Teresa de Jesus*, captained by Dom Filipe Lobo, and on this ship the Viceroy sailed. *Santa Teresa* was seconded in rank by vice-flagship (*Almiranta*) *São José*, under the orders of Captain Dom Francisco Mascarenhas; the *nau São Carlos* under the command of Francisco Lobo; and the *nau São Tomé* with Nuno Pereira as Captain. The galleons São Salvador and Trinidade with Gonçalo de Sequeira de Sousa and Sancho de Tovar da Silva respectively as Captains were also part of this fleet, as well as two *patachos* under the orders of Francisco de Sodré Pereira and Francisco Cardoso de Almeida (*Boxer*, 1930, p.6).

Dom Francisco da Gama was born in 1565 as the son of Vasco da Gama, third Count of Vidigueira, and great-grandson of the famous navigator who, after discovering the sea route to India, became India's second Viceroy. At the age of thirteen, he was part, with his father, of King Sebastião's fateful North Africa campaign. He fought by his side and saw his father killed; he was himself made prisoner.

He was ransomed in 1595 and returned to Lisbon. Early in the following year he was appointed 16th Viceroy of India, replacing Matias de Albuquerque, and took his post in Goa, capital of Portuguese India, on May 22nd 1597. For three years he performed his government duties under quite difficult circumstances such as lack of funds and ships, and the constant threat from the English in the South and the Mongols in the North. As ingrained corruption reached deplorable proportions, he was forced to undertake deep reforms.

However, the rigor he imposed and the military victories he obtained were not enough to avoid deep uneasiness surrounding his administration and controversial personality. Twenty-two years had passed since his return from India when he left Lisbon in the fleet, again headed for Goa.

During the voyage, the crew of *São José* was afflicted by disease, which also infected the Captain and Pilot. With communication with the other ships very poor, the *São José*, which sailed last, fell unusually far behind the other ships. On the night of 22nd July as the four ships sailed off Mogincual, approaching the Isle of Mozambique, the six ships of the Anglo-Dutch "Fleet of Defense" attacked. The Anglo-Dutch fleet attacked the *São José* with four ships, which was not difficult as her isolated position made her an easier target.

The four ships turned their cannon at the *São José*, while a ship sailing more to the North intercepted the *São Carlos* as she turned to come to the distressed vice-flagship's rescue. Both ships fought all night and the morning of the 23rd against the Anglo-Dutch fleet but, by the end of the day, the *São José* virtually stopped all resistance.

With the Captain sick and the Pilot fallen in combat, the ship itself badly damaged by enemy fire, most of her sails torn to pieces – indeed her main mast broken – the crew decided to go ashore in a desperate attempt to escape the enemy and gain some time to repair the ship. However, in the process of retreating to land, a reef in Mogincual (known nowadays as Infusse) blocked the passage. The *São José* hit the crest of the reef, lost the rudder and was completely out of control [1]. In a last attempt to stop the ship the crew dropped anchors, but she was dragged to deeper waters off the coast, where the ship finally broke apart and sank the day after.

The Anglo-Dutch fleet, assured of the tragic end of the *São José*, decided to chase the *Santa Teresa* and the *São Carlos*, leaving only one of their ships to oversee her. In a merciless pursuit, the fleet followed them up to the entry of the Isle of Mozambique. There, fearing the fire-power of *São Sebastião* fort, they decided to turn back and safely plunder the spoils of the *São José*.

For some obscure reason, the *Santa Teresa* and the *São Carlos* had already passed by the islet of Goa when they ran aground on a sandbank (today known as *"Banco de São Lourenço"*), quite close to the comforting protection of *São Sebastião* fort. Meanwhile the Anglo-Dutch fleet sailed back to Mogincual where the majority of the survivors of the *São José* were made prisoners and all the cargo they could lay their hands on was plundered. Reports from the time mention one hundred prisoners and three or four hundred drowned as well as the loss of a significant part of the precious cargo (*BNL*, Reservados – cx. 26, no 153).

After this fateful episode, Dom Francisco da Gama eventually reached Goa, quite some time after the surviving ships that had sailed with the fleet. For six years Dom Francisco administered the Portuguese territories of India; but his reputation and the powerful intrigues mounted by his many enemies eventually got the better of him and all his possessions were seized by the Crown. In 1628 he received the order to hand the government to the Bishop of Cochin and returned to Europe in disgrace. He died at Oropesa in 1632 on his way to Madrid where it is thought he was going to try to prove his innocence to the Court and King Filipe the Third of Portugal.

FIG.1
Old painting of the Island of Mozambique by Lisuarte de Abreu.

FIG. 2
The cannons of the São Sebastião fort with the islet of Goa at the foreground.

(1) Most of the information about this battle was collected from the *"Itinerário do Padre Jerónimo Lobo"* (BNL, F.G. 1540 – flo 127 / 128vo), but after the excavation phase this particular quote proved to be inaccurate as the rudder was found with part of the hull some 3 km to the NW of the reef. Most probably they lost *control* on the rudder rather than losing the rudder itself.

The wreck site and excavation of the coins

Based on archival accounts of the battle, a group of archaeologists from Arqueonautas Worldwide S.A. started a wide remote sensing survey in the area of Mogincual with the objective of locating the remains of the vice-flagship of the 1622 fleet.

The site was found on the 27th of September 2004, during systematic magnetometer and visual surveys on Infusse shoal. The main part of the wreck site was located in the Northwest side of Infusse reef at a depth of 21.5m on a seabed of sand and loose rocks. (Fig.3)

The objects exposed on the seabed at first inspection were three bronze cannons, five iron cannons, a rudder pintle and seven anchors. The debris field of the wreck had a length of 4530m from anchor A2 to anchor A8, following a coherent direction SSE-NNW with the predominant winds and swell in this geographical area (Fig.4).

During the pre-disturbance survey, an area of 120m^2 (10 x 12m) with a concentration of silver coins was located between anchors A6 and A7 and cannons G6 and G7.

Excavation began on 06 May 2005 and continued during the seasons of 2006 and 2007. The team largely consisted of divers, IT-specialists and archaeologists, all with vast experience in marine archaeological field work. The first objective was to establish a web of permanent datum points which would permit the precise mapping of the terrain and the wreck remains. After a detailed survey and careful reflection, an area was established where cultural debris was observed, either exposed on the seabed or buried in the sediment but within the reach of the metal detectors, to deploy our grid system for the excavation phase.

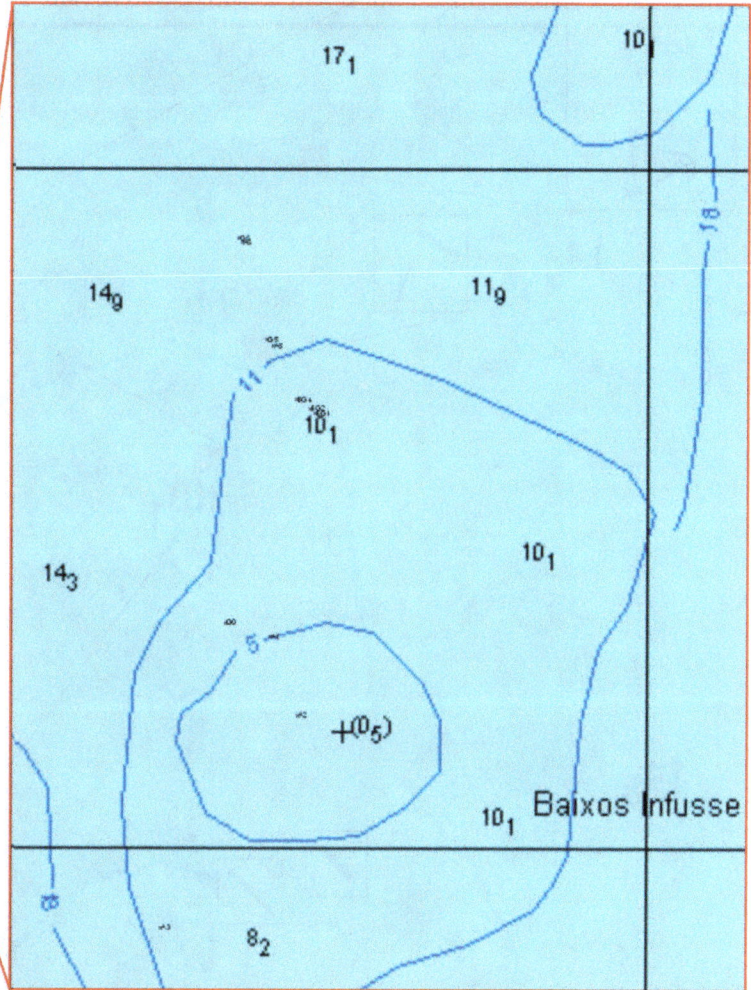

FIG.3
Geographical location of
Infusse shoal off the coast of
Mozambique.

13

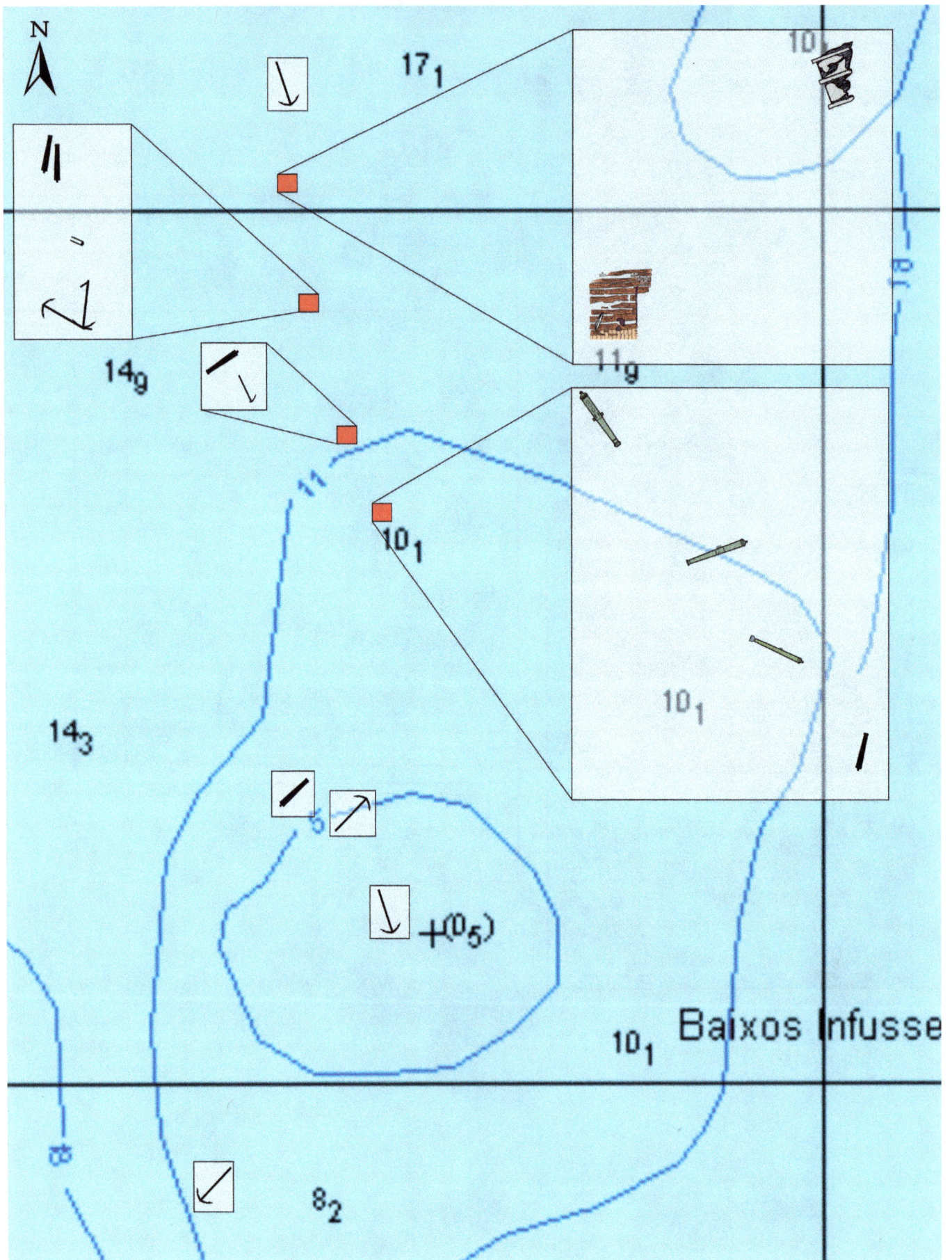

FIG.4
Debris field of the *São José* wreck site. The second red square from the top is the area where all the silver coins were found. The distance from the southernmost anchor to the northernmost anchor is 4530m.

The adopted grid system was of 24 grids (5 x 5m, 25m^2) orientated North-South and East-West, covering the entire area with visible cultural material. The grids were built with white plastic rope, 8mm in diameter, and marked every meter with a small plastic tag; at every 5m (beginnings, ends and intersections) the line was also marked in black for easy reference. The fixing points for this datum grid were plastic bags filled with sand and stones in order to avoid unnecessary contamination of the area with modern objects such as lead weights or steel rods. The entire area prepared for excavation covered 750m^2. Sediment was removed by using a water dredge controlled by the divers. All silver coins were found buried in the sediment, at depths varying from 0.15m to 1m in a few of the cases. From the central nucleus of these artefacts (eastern edge of S18 and western edge of S19), where the concentration of heavy clumps was located, the scattering covered a radius of approximately 5m in every direction, where the loose coins were located as a layer 0.2m thick (*Mirabal*, 2006) *(Fig.5)*.

Unique artefact numbers were given to every item or concreted group of items. Each artefact number was allocated to a group of coins found in a specific area, providing this way the exact location from where the coins were recovered.

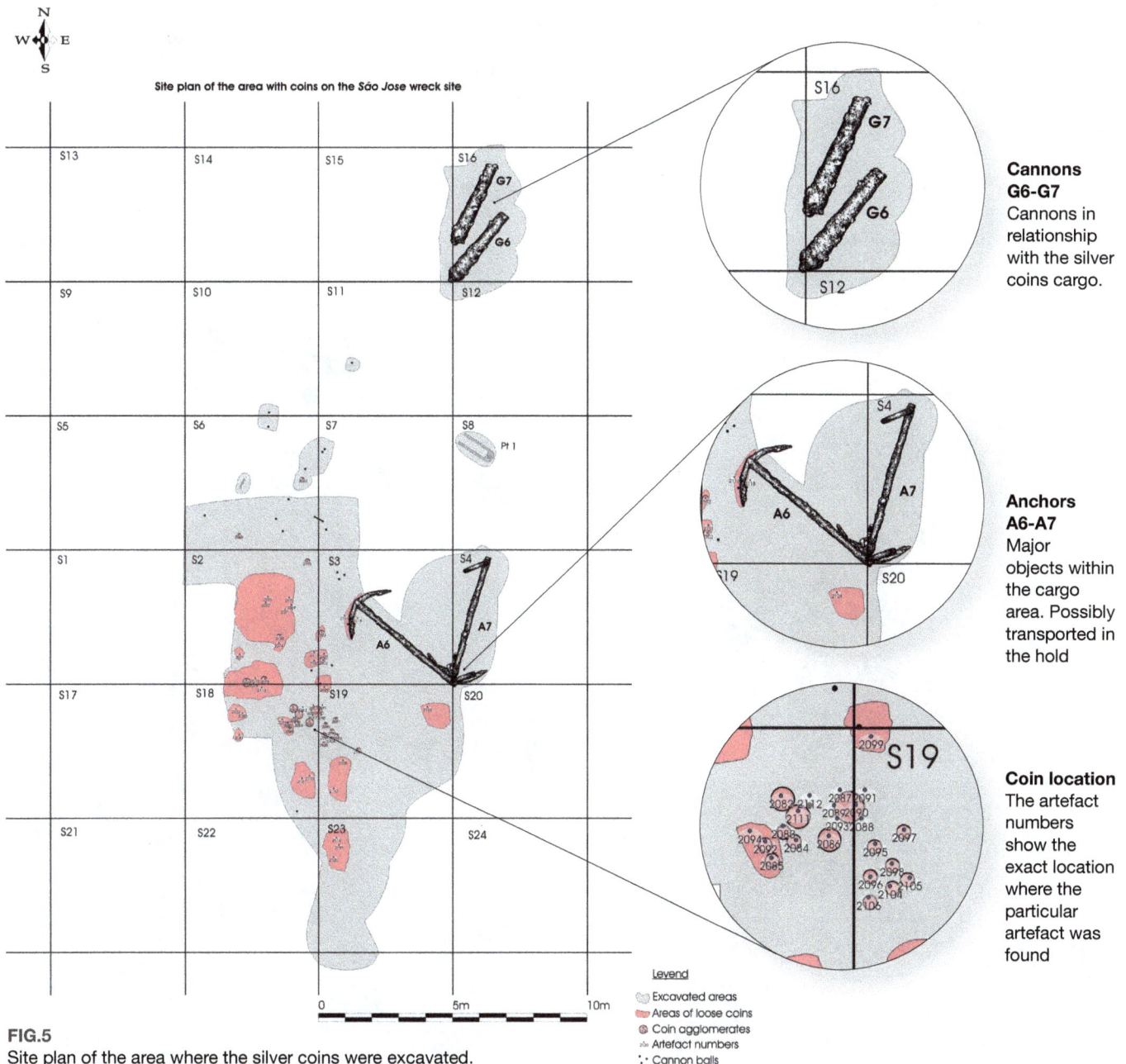

FIG.5
Site plan of the area where the silver coins were excavated.

15

FIG.6-22
Excavation operations at the wreck site.

FIG.7

FIG.8

FIG.9

FIG.10

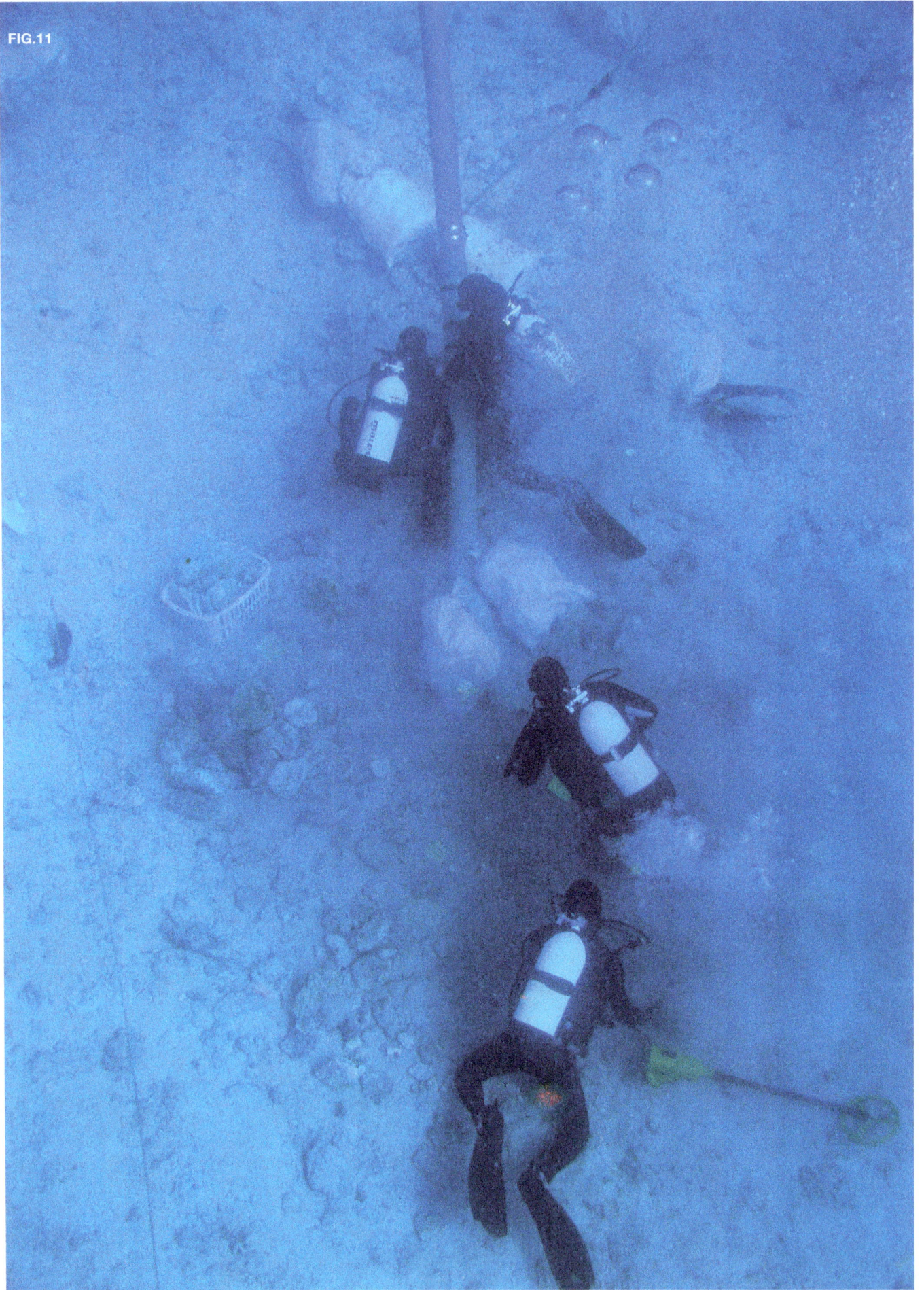

FIG.11

Once an artefact number, containing various numbers of items, was stabilized in the laboratory, the coins from its content were catalogued individually in three groups as follows:

Numismatic coins
All pieces with information (mintmarks, assayer marks, etc.) that could help in their study and identification.

Eroded coins
All pieces without marks but still with the shape and features of a coin. In most of the eroded coins the geographical area of origin is recognizable.

Washers
All pieces that have lost all information on them and have become a thin sheet of silver.

All numismatic coins were individually introduced in the Access database prepared for that purpose, with each coin acquiring an individual number rooted on the artefact number from which it belongs. That is to say, the coins from artefact 2085 (a "cluster") were numbered 2085.001, 2085.002, etc.

FIG.12

FIG.13

FIG.14

FIG.15

FIG.16

FIG.17

FIG.18

21

FIG.19

FIG.20

FIG.21

FIG.22

The coins

From the total volume of coins excavated from the *nau Almiranta São José*, estimated at 23,211; a group of 7,525 have been studied, divided into 4,390 (59%) of 8 *reales*, 3,120 (41%) of 4 *reales* and 15 (0,2%) of 2 reales (Fig.23).

All are Hispanic coins, hammer-struck during the Spanish kingdoms of Felipe II (1556-1598), Felipe III (1598-1621) and Felipe IV (1621-1665) and follow the design established by the so-called *Pragmáticas de la Nueva Estampa* (New Engraving Rules), as determined by Felipe II in 1566 and put into practice in the Spanish colonies from 1572.

There may be an exception in just one coin. The case of artefact 2072.094 which is a poor quality coin and difficult to see the markings, but a numismatist colleague noted it as possibly being an *early Segovia screw-press coin* (*Tedesco*, 2008). According to the design of the New Engraving, the obverse side of the coin includes the shield of the House of Habsburg, which contains the arms of the territories under the Spanish crown. The arms of Castile, Leon, Aragon and Naples-Sicily appear in the top half, whilst the arms of Austria, modern Burgundy, old Burgundy and Brabant appear on the bottom half and the arms of Flanders and Tyrol in a small shield in the centre. A small pomegranate centred in the upper and lower half symbolises the Kingdom of Granada, the last Moorish possession in Spain reconquered by the Catholic Kings in 1492. The reverse side of the coin displays the quartered cross with the alternating arms of Castile and Leon, encir- cled by a double border with 8 lobes (*Díaz*, 2008).

Coin distribution by denominations

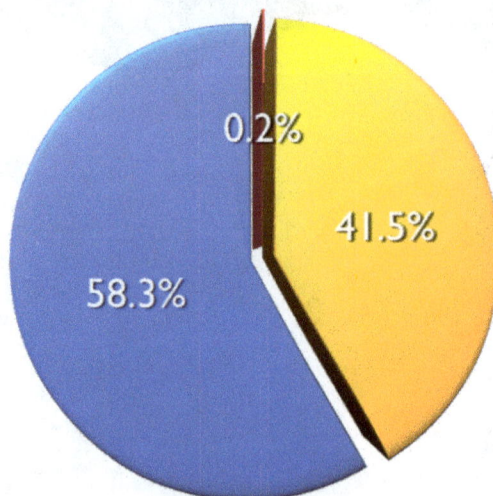

0.2%

41.5%

58.3%

FIG.23
Amounts and percentages for the different denominations within the Numismatics' coins sample.

● 2 Reales (15)   ● 4 Reales (3120)   ● 8 Reales (4390)

According to the same royal statute, the external inscription, which starts on the obverse and finishes on the reverse, generally reads: PHILIPVS II (III or IIII, depending on the case) DEI GRATIA HISPANIARVM REX, and D.G. HISPANIARUM ET INDIARUM REX.

The geographical distribution includes 3 groups:

- Coins minted in Mexico, Viceroyalty of New Spain: 2,974 coins (39%)

- Coins made in mints of metropolis Spain: 2,537 (34%)

- Coins from Lima and Potosí, Viceroyalty of Perú: 2,014 (27%) *(Fig.24)*.

Coin distribution by countries

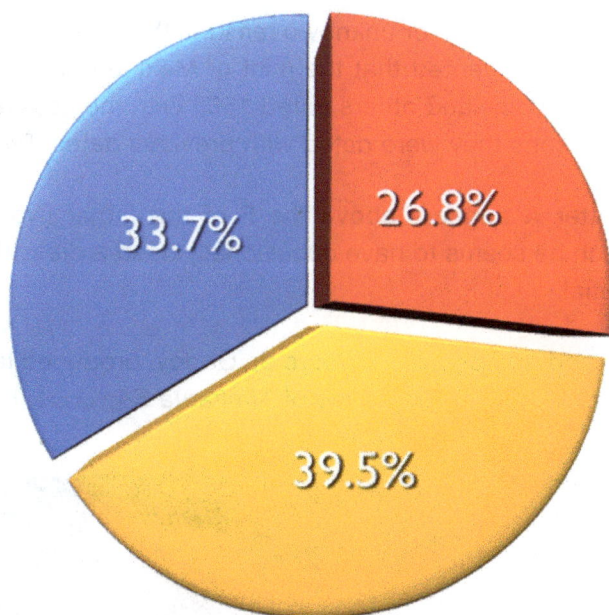

33.7% 26.8% 39.5%

● Peru (2014)   ● Mexico (2974)   ● Spain (2537)

FIG.24
Amounts and percentages for the different mint countries within the Numismatics' coins sample.

MEXICAN COINS

The Mexican mint, founded by Charles I in 1535, was the first to be es- tablished by the colonizers of the new world. Amongst these coins from Mexico only 7 correspond to the assayer with the initial **O** [Bernardo de Oñate, 1564-1589]. He had been working in the Mexican mint since the times of Charles I and his mother Iohana and still had the same position when coins of the new Habsburg shield design started to be struck in the mint in 1572. Some references indicate that in the mid-1580s he was replaced by Luis de Oñate [1578-1589] who may have been his son. The coins continued to be produced with the same initial **O**, hence there are no other elements that enable one to recognize the differences between coins of both assayers.

The coins minted in Mexico are distributed (by assayer) as follows:

- 7 of assayer **O** [Bernardo de Oñate, 1564-1589 and/or Luis de Oñate (possibly Bernardo's son) 1578-1589]

- 557 of assayer **F** [Francisco de Morales, 1589-1608 and 1610-1618]

- 23 of assayer **A** [Antonio de Morales, son of the former, 1608-1610]

- 972 of assayer **D** [Diego de Godoy, 1618-1634]

- 1,415 undetermined as one cannot see the assayer's mark.

Dates only started to be struck on coins in Mexico from 1607 onwards, with the Francisco de Morales' production. The date 1600, which appears on some coins of assayer **A** (No. 2095.091 and 2095.225) therefore cannot be trusted, for it is known that this official worked at the mint during a period of his father's absence, between 1608 and 1610. It is possible that there was a mistake in the manufacture of dies, perhaps unnoticed by the assayer, which resulted in the date 1600 *(Fig.25)*.

These coins are quite well-known, but it is accepted that for unknown reasons they were made between 1608 and 1610 but struck with the 1600 date. As it is accepted that the mint of Mexico only began to use dates on the coins in 1607, it is considered that these coins and others dated 1603 with the assayer's mark **F**, were made after 1607, although for inexplicable reasons they were dated with previous dates *(Proctor, 2006)*.

On a different coin by this assayer, the letter **A** appears above the **F** of the father (No. 2104.242, **A/F**), confirming his temporary labour, during which he seems to have occasionally used a die with the initial of his father upon which he overstruck his own initial.

It is worth noting that Francisco de Morales and his successor, Diego de Godoy, produced large quantities of coins, demonstrated by the high volume of their coins in the cargo of *Almiranta São José*. It also seems that

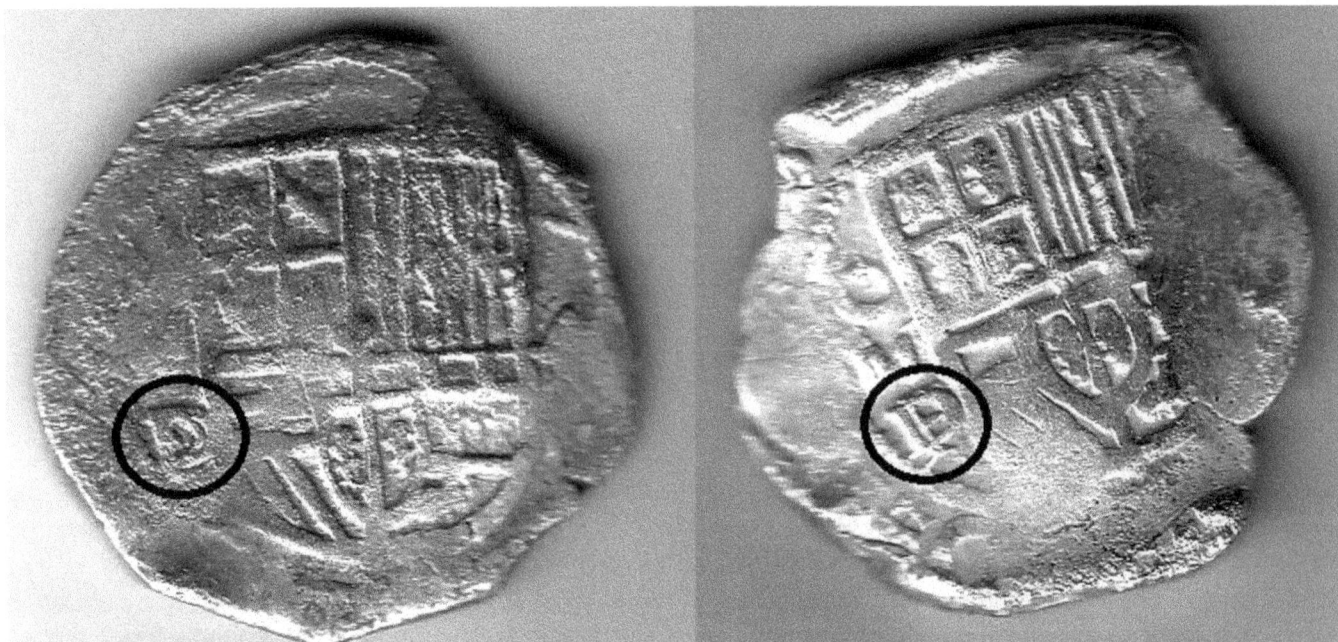

FIG.25
Coin number 2080.028 (left) showing assayer mark "D" over "F" and coin number 2070.042 (right) with the variant "F" over "D".

FIG.26
Coin number 2095.225 showing the assayer mark "A" with struck date of "1600". The date is located in the upper left side of the coin.

at some point the latter replaced the former for some time and used **F** dies marking them with his initial **D**. When the former returned to his post, he also used the die of the latter, which had the initial **D**, with a letter **F** over-struck by the returning assayer. This procedure was common in Spanish mints, especially in Mexico and Potosi, and in this case it resulted in the assayer mark **D/F** (No. 2080.028) and **F/D** (No. 2070.042). Amongst the studied coins there are various with these characteristics *(Fig.26)*.

One extremely rare variant of this situation is found on a coin with both assayers' marks in the obverse, **F** on the left side and **D** on the right side (No. 2089.006) *(Fig.27)*.

It is somehow puzzling to see that three coins among the Mexican mint marked by assayer **D** [attributed to Diego de Godoy, 1618-1634] had a date stamped that reads "1611" (2081.066, 2097.036 and 2124.000). This date is completely out of the published range of years in which supposedly Diego de Godoy worked at the Mexican mint. The close trimming could mean the dates also read as "1617" but that would also be out of the period of work of this assayer *(Fig.28)*.

Within the large sample of Mexican coins recovered from this wreck site there is one coin that immediately catches ones attention: No. 2123.202. This badly eroded 4 *reales* Mexican coin still shows a very distinct "1621" date *(Fig.29)*.

Nowadays, with the development of transport means and communication, it is not surprising for an object produced in Mexico to appear in some other part of the world within days, or even hours, of its production; but back in the 17th century it would seem quite unlikely that a coin stamped in Mexico in 1621 ended up in the waters of Mozambique on July of 1622, having first passed through Spain and Portugal. Although mathematically possible it seemed to us far-fetched, considering the weather-related delays of the Spanish fleets and the consequent transportation of the silver from Seville to Lisbon.

The Spanish fleet collected the silver and other goods at the *"Feria de Portobelo"*, Panama, during the month of June and normally the transactions took place for more than three weeks. For instance, the fleet of 1624 which arrived in Portobelo on 19 June that year took only three weeks to load the cargo in their holds and resume the trip to Cartagena, La Habana and then to Spain.

Probably the answer to our doubts lies in a letter from General Larraspuru, who arrived in Spain in 1621, in which he refers that that year the silver was collected in only 17 days *"something that had never been done so fast"* (*AGI*, Indef. , 1142).

The presence of this "1621" coin within the cargo of the *São José* provides a quick but self-explanatory glimpse at the celerity of the financial flow between the Americas, Europe and the East in the 17th century.

FIG.27
Coin number 2089.006 showing two assayer marks "F" on the left and "D" on the right. This is a very rare coin.

FIG.28
Coin number 2097.036 showing the struck date of "1611" and the assayer mark "D".

FIG.29
The "fast" Mexican coin (number 2123.202) which made it all the way from Mexico to Mozambique in less than one year passing first by Spain and Portugal.

SPANISH COINS

The second largest volume of analysed coins, a total of 2,537, includes 1,503 undetermined ones with no visible mintmark and thus difficult to identify. The remaining 1,034 coins are distributed between the coins from Seville (774), Toledo (239), Granada (9), Segovia (7) and Madrid (5).

It is understandable that coins struck in Spain were produced with higher quality than the ones from the Spanish-American mints, despite being hammer-struck, due to the care and experience of the manufacturers who produced them.

At the time, the largest mint in the Iberian Peninsula was in Seville, which justifies the larger amount of pieces originating from there found amongst the *São José* cargo. The second largest amount in the studied collection comes from Toledo especially when compared to the meagre samples from the other three Spanish mints.

The Seville coins are broken down in chronological order, as follows:

- 1 of assayer **H** [Hernando de Rojas, 1590-1591]

- 49 of assayer **B** [Juan Vicente Bravo, 1592-1597]

- 70 of assayer **V** [Juan Bautista Veyntín, 1611-1619]

- 273 of assayer **D** [Domínguez Ortiz, 1612-1615]

- 156 of assayer **G** [Gaspar de Talavera, 1615-1621]

- 225 undetermined as there is no visible stamp by the assayer.

One particular coin of assayer **H** (No. 2096.142) calls for special attention because it displays the date 1590, allowing it to be identified as a Hernando de Rojas production, despite the fact that other succeeding assayers were also called Hernando and used the same initial *(Fig.30)*.

A curiosity was a coin minted in Seville by assayer **G**, Gaspar de Talavera, dated 1620, found with a denomination of 2 *reales* struck on the coin and a weight of 4 *reales*, which is no doubt an error (No. 2084.076). Similar errors have been observed on several occasions, but what makes this coin of particular interest is that it is more common to find the opposite, that is to say, coins of smaller denominations with stamps of higher denominations (i.e. a coin of 4 *reales* weight with a stamp of 8 *reales*). In the case of this coin, it seems that it was very thick and despite the trimming it had to be left as 4 *reales* regardless of the 2 *reales* stamp.

The pieces from the mint in Toledo amount to 239, distributed as follows:

- 1 of assayer **M** [Eugenio de Manzanas, 1566?-1593]

- 1 of assayer **M** in a circle [Alejo de Montoya, 1591-1598]

- 44 of assayer **C** [Melchor Rodríguez del Castillo, 1599-1616] • 34

  of assayer **V** [unknown, 1611-1618]

- 89 of assayer **P** [unknown, 1615 and 1619-1621]

- 70 undetermined.

A 1572 document illustrates that Eugenio de Manzanas was assayer of the Toledo mint and that he had worked some time before with his relative Baltasar de Manzanas who used the same initial; however, he had not minted coins with the New Engraving, but rather used an earlier type, with the Fernando and Isabel names *(Pellicer, 1997)*.

A reference found in this study's bibliography mentions that Melchor Rodríguez del Castillo was assayer of the Toledo mint between 1593 and 1595, and that afterwards he transferred to Segovia, where he held the same position between 1599 and 1611 *(Idem)*. However, among the coins dated between 1609 and 1611 that were studied (No. 2080.051, 2095.397, 2095.500), there are some pieces from Toledo with the initial **C**, which cannot be attributed to any other assayer of that mint, leading one to assume that during these years the assayer returned to Toledo, or that he worked temporarily at both mints.

FIG.30
Coin from assayer "H" dated "1590" (number 2096.142) The date is visible on the right side of the shield.

FIG.31
Coin from Segovia showing the Portuguese arms. Art. Number 2101.122.

An interesting aspect that is common to the seven coins from the Segovia mint is a small shield with the arms of Portugal, centred on the two upper quadrants within the Habsburg shield *(Fig.29)*.

Portugal was part of the Spanish domain between 1580 and 1640, but for coins minted in America the New Engraving Rules had special characteristics, like never including the arms of Portugal. An exception confirming this rule was the new world Santa Fé de Bogotá mint that although it did not begin producing until 1622, it did include the Portuguese arms.

From this collection of coins, two are associated to two assayers who worked together and united their initials in the form of the mark **IM** [Ioan de Ortega and Ioan de Morales, 1585-1590]; one of these coins has a partial date 159? (No. 2101.271). Another coin shows the initial **I** [Ioan de Ortega, working alone, 1590-1598]. In one case, there is the particularity that an **O** appears over the I (No. 2089.049). Although this is not mentioned in any of the sources listed in the bibliography, the **O** may have been added by the assayer Ortega to establish a clearer difference with the joint mark of his predecessors Morales or, most probably, it belonged to the Valladolid mint which has a similar assayer mark circa 1620. Lastly, two other coins correspond to assayer **A** [Andrés de Pedrera, 1617-1621].

Of the remaining Spanish coins, five belong to the Madrid mint, one of assayer **G** [Gonzalo Rodríguez Bermúdez, 1615-1621] and four of assayer **V** [Juan Velázquez, 1621-1628]. Another nine are from the Granada mint, eight from the production of assayer **M** [Francisco Mínguez, 1597-1621]. None of these coins display any particularities.

PERUVIAN COINS

Among the collection of coins minted in Peru, the third group in terms of quantity, a small lot of eleven exemplars originate from the Lima mint, the capital of the Viceroyalty. The Lima mint was founded by Felipe II in 1565 and started to operate three years later. In 1573 it was closed due to irregularities detected in the operations and transferred to the city of Chuquisaca (today named Sucre, in Bolivia), baptised as La Plata by the Spaniards after locating important silver deposits nearby. Shortly afterwards, the mint was relocated to Lima and operated until 1588, closing again until the second half of the following century. It is because of these inconsistencies that the production during the 16th Century was so limited, explaining the scarcity of these coins in the *São José* cargo when compared to the significant abundance of coins from Potosí.

One of the coins is attributed to assayer **L**, who only worked in 1577, but his name is unknown and there are also doubts as to whether he had worked in Potosi rather than Lima. The remaining nine correspond to assayer **D** [Diego de la Torre, 1577-1588]. This assayer is well known thanks to the high quality of his coins, considered the best silver coining of the 16th Century in the whole of Spanish America. The obverse side of six of the Lima coins, (2078.016, 2081.270, 2097.078, 2106.000, 2122.014, 2123.175) catch one's attention because of a small six-pointed star, believed to have been included by the assayer in order to identify the coins from Lima, because both this mint and that of Potosí used the letter **P**; in these pieces made in Lima the **P** refers to Peru although some specialists have suggested that the star was in commemoration of the Epiphany (*Tedesco*, 2008) *(Fig.32)*.

FIG.32
Coin from the Lima mint, assayer "D" with the six point star over the assayer mark. Art. Number 2078.016.

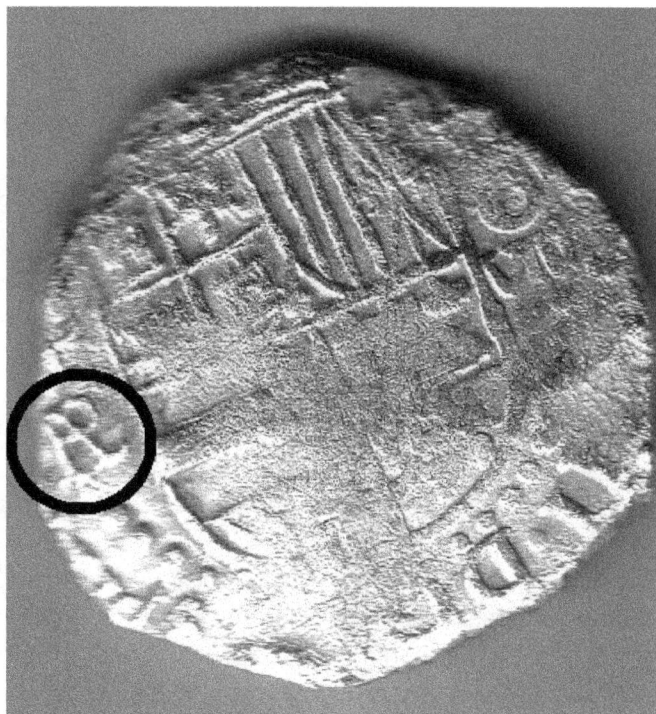

FIG.33
Assayer mark "RAL" coin from the Potosi mint. Art. Number 2099.071.

31

In 1574 Felipe II founded the *"Villa Imperial de Potosí"* mint next to the largest silver deposit in Spanish America known as *"Cerro Rico"*. During the colonial era, *"Cerro Rico"* enriched the Spanish crown with the colossal sum of approximately 2,000 million *"onzas"* of silver (pieces of 8 *reales*), resulting in the development of the Renaissance in Europe and contributing to the financing for the construction of the *"Armada Invencible"*. The silver also turned Potosí into an immensely prosperous city, rumoured to have *"paved its streets with silver tiles."* (Barrón, 2000).

The wealth of the city was eccentric. The celebrations for the coronation of Felipe II cost more than 8,000,000 *pesos*. Women spent between 12 and 14,000 *pesos* on jewelry and clothes during the festivities and it is known that a lady from Potosi spent 500 *pesos* just on pearls. Even the *"indios"* wore clothes embroidered with pearls and precious stones *(Cobb, 1945)*.

An account written in the early 17th century, the anonymous *Descripción del Virreinato del Perú*, probably by a Jewish merchant addressed to the Dutch, reads the following:

"...y se hacen de seis hasta 7,000 mil barras todos los años, y unas por otras valen 1,000 pesos. Y hacen grandes sumas de reales y se deshace mucha plata para vajilla, y hay más de ochenta años que se descubrió esta mina y se tiene sacado de ella y se saca cada día una suma infinita de plata" (AAVV, 1965)

(... and there are made from six until 7,000 thousand ingots every year, and one and other worth 1,000 *pesos*. And they make large sums of *reales* and a lot of silver is melted for tableware, and there had been more than eighty years that this mine was found and it had been extracted and continue extracting every day an infinite sum of silver) (author's translation)

The 2,014 coins minted in Potosí are distributed (by assayer) as follows:

- 2 of assayer **A** [Juan Alvarez Reinaltes, 1586-1589]

- 129 of assayer **B** [Juan Ballesteros Narváez, 1581-1586, and his

  brother Hernando Ballesteros, 1589-1598 and 1598-1605/10]

- 269 of assayer **R** [Baltasar Ramos Leceta, 1590-1598 and 1598-1610/ 13]

- 357 of assayer **Q** [Agustín de la Quadra, 1613-1616]

- 157 of assayer **M** [Juan Muñoz, 1616-1617]

- 176 of assayer **T** [Juan Ximénez de Tapia, 1618-1623]

- 926 undetermined as one cannot see the assayer's mark.

The coins from the Potosí mint often displayed certain peculiarities due to the extraordinary production and the industriousness which was often necessary to strike coins. The work of Alonso López de Barriales and Juan Alvarez Reinaltes mentioned above, coincided in some years, both using the initial **A**, without establishing their own elements or characteristics to differentiate the coins.

Juan Ballesteros Narváez was the most productive assayer, although on some occasions he was replaced by his brother Hernando. They produced a large quantity of coins which occasionally included small details in the design that may allow us to define the period during which they were struck. In the analysed pieces, however, it has not been possible to detect such characteristics due to the increased level of deterioration and erosion resulting from over 380 years in a marine environment.

Baltasar Ramos Leceta worked on some occasions as a tenant of Juan Ballesteros, using the letter **R** with a slanted diagonal line; subsequently, during the kingdom of Felipe III, he modified his initial by making the line curved. The coins from the studied collection come from this second period, when coins from Potosí started to be dated.

Five of these pieces exceptionally display the monogram **RAL**, formed by superimposing all three letters, estimated to have been made by the assayer in 1618 (No. 2074.036, 2099.071, 2105.026, 2121.186, 2122.008). These coins are considered rare *(Fig.33)*.

Ramos Leceta was followed by Agustín de la Quadra [1613-1616] (No. 2097.060, the best piece among the Potosí collection). This assayer sometimes used dies from his predecessors, over-struck with an initial **Q**, which produced the rare variant **Q/R** (No. 2104.047), of which only seven have been found. Even more unusual ones include the following mint marks - the inverted **Q** mark (No. 2092.001), a double **Q** (No. 2096.228), a double **P** (No. 2120.113) and another coin with a **P** twice its usual size (No. 2120.079). All the aforementioned variants are rare. The next assayer was Juan Muñoz and, following tradition, he also used dies by the former official, which were thus marked **M/Q** (No. 2078.097). This is also a rare and scarce variant observed on only three of the studied coins *(Fig.34)*.

FIG.34
Variants in the Potosi mint coins (from left to right upper row): Q/R (No. 2104.047), inverted Q (No. 2092.001) and double Q (No. 2096.228). From left to right (lower row): Double P as mintmark (No. 2120.113), P twice its usual size (No. 2120.079) and M/Q (No. 2078.097).

The last assayer in this group is Juan Ximénez de Tapia. This assayer's coins are characterized by a series of errors and deficiencies due to poor workmanship. In some of the studied coins it is noted that the blundered strike results in the quadrant of one shield overlapping the others (e.g. No. 2081.298). There were also other examples of coins struck with a faulty die. Twelve of these coins are particularly noteworthy because the upper quadrants of the shield appear transposed, that is to say Naples-Sicily and Aragon to the left, and Castile and Leon to the right (No. 2080.085) *(Fig.35) (Fig.36)*.

FIG.35
Overlapping quadrants of the shield (No. 2081.298).

FIG.36
Transposed quadrants of the shield (No. 2080.085).

A document from 1616 *(Sellschopp, 1971)* narrates the visit of the inspectors, which took place that year at the Potosí mint. Several samples of the accumulated dies over several years were analysed, leading to the conclusion that coins by Baltasar Ramos Leceta and Agustín de la Quadra displayed considerable errors in weight and fineness or silver content, thus they were seemingly fraudulent. The assayers were no longer alive to react to the claim. Among the coins from the São José, those that are 8 reales predominantly weigh between 20 and 27gr, despite the deterioration and the natural erosion caused by the sea. However, some of these coins weigh between 11 and 16gr; one can thus assume that they probably weighed less even on the day they were struck. This disproportion is not only found in the aforementioned assayers, but also in other officials of the mint *(Table 1)*

ARTEFACT NUMBER	ASSAYER	ACTUAL WEIGHT (gr)
2156.000	R	12
2114.067	Q	13
2114.026	B	14
2104.378	M	11
2110.127	T	14

TABLE 1
Coin weight by Assayer

Metallurgic analysis applied

Two sample lots of the most eroded coins ("washers"), excavated from the *São José* wreck, and were selected for metallurgical analysis. The analysis was done using the non-destructive Semi-Quantitative X-Ray diffraction method, conducted by Ledoux & Company of Teaneck, NJ, USA. The results were the following:

Lot # 1982010-001

Silver	97.4%
Copper	2.0%
Lead	0.4%
Mercury	0.1%

Lot # 1982010-002

Silver	94.5%
Copper	5.2%
Mercury	0.2%

Besides the high content of silver, which validates the quality of the coinage produced in the New World, it is worth noting the traces of mercury in the metal. The presence of mercury confirms that when these coins were produced, the process of amalgamation of the silver used was the "Patio Process" *(Proceso de Patio)*. This process was introduced in New Spain by Bartolomé de Medina in 1555, and although the supply of mercury from Spain was not always available, it appears that, by the end of the 16th century, this situation had been resolved *(Bargalló, 1955)*.

The cargo of the São José

Like most of the outward-bound Portuguese Indiamen of the 17th century, the *São José* was carrying money in the form of silver coins to buy goods in Asia, mainly pepper and other spices. As the original cargo manifest of this ship hasn't been found in the archives there are many speculations regarding the exact amount of money that was lost in the wreckage and even more about the actual amount of silver transported on the ship. Nevertheless, using the documental sources and the results of the archaeological excavation of the wreck, we can calculate this with a certain degree of accuracy. Some of the archival documents studied state:

"From the rear Admiral was saved part of the King's money, nothing from private merchants, and even the orphans of the King were taken by the enemy as well as many prisoners" (T. of the A). *"Da nao almirante se salvou parte do cabedal del Rei, e nenhum das partes, e ate as órfãs del Rei levarão os inimigos e muita outra gente cativa"* (BNL, Reservados – cx. 26, nº 156).

Another Portuguese document is more detailed and states that since the boat was damaged, the rescue operation took longer than expected but it was possible to rescue 68,000 *cruzados* from the Crown and some from private traders and 124 people; the enemies only captured the little that remained on board. *"como llevava el batel destroçado gasto mucho tiempo en adereçarle mas salvaranse 68,000 cruzados, del Rey y otra plata de partes e algunas 124 personas de toda suerte"; "los inimigos se avian apoderado desto poco que quedo en la nave"* (DUP, 1962, vol. 2, pp. 503-504). This document also mentions that "680,000 *cruzados* from the King were saved from the wreckage", but this must be a transcription error.

The English version says that they recovered 68,553 *cruzados* and split this amount between their four ships (Ball, 1622, pp. 132-210).

From the Portuguese archives we can assume that at least *18,000 cruzados* were on board when the ship sank; from a letter of the Vice-King dated March 11, 1624 *(BNL, Fondo General, 1817)* "nine chests of silver with 18,000 cruzados were lost".

Another document states not only what was lost with the *São José* but also what arrived at Goa from that fleet. *"o cabedal que ia nas 3 naus da vossa companhia chegou a salvamento, e que do que levava a S. José que fez naufrágio em Mogincual, se perderam só 9 caixões em que iam 18,000 cruzados e ficaram líquidos 142,000 cruzados, que são 284,000 xerafins"* (AHU, India, cx.15, no 177, fl. 5v). "9 chests with a total of *18,000 cruzados* were lost in the *São José*; the remaining money in the *São José* as well as in the other naus was rescued totalling *142,000 cruzados*"

The way in which money was transported on these ships has always been a subject of interest for researchers and the public in general. What did the legendary "treasure chests" actually looked like? Were they like those seen in the pirate movies, with a shiny mixture of gold coins, silver coins, jewellery and pearls? How big and heavy were they? With this study of the *São José* cargo of silver coins we will try to shed some light on this interesting subject.

Before the archaeological excavation of the *São José* we could only calculate this based on a few compilations and studies by historians and even fewer historical documents.

When trying to study and understand the Portuguese *"Carreira da India"* it is almost unavoidable to consult the works of Professor Vitorino Magalhães Godinho, who had possibly made the most thorough research on the circulation of money and merchandise, including precious metals and eastern spices following the Portuguese maritime discoveries.

«*A Rota do cabo: o triunfo dos reales*» (*Godinho*, 1981-1983a) is a chapter from one of his books that offers a perceptive insight into this enormous change, which took place during the second half of the 16th century. The introduction of Mexican-Peruvian silver minted as *reales* into Spain turned this new coin into the main merchandise exported for the trade of far eastern spices. The following extracts are from his works:

Quantity of *reales* sent from Lisbon and arriving at Goa and Cochin for the purchase of pepper, end of the 16th – beginning of 17th centuries (value in *cruzados* of 10 *reales* each) (Table 2)

The value of the purchases is always expressed in monetary units of gold, *cruzados* or *ducados*, which served as the lead currency for calculations, but payments were always made with silver coins, equivalent in Spain to 8.8 *reales* or 1 *cruzado* (*Idem*).

The money that was sent annually from Lisbon to the *"Casa da Índia"* to pay for the eastern spices was estimated at 200,000 *cruzados* in a 1618 document, a value that is consistent with the data in the following table, relating only to the pepper trade.

DATE	VALUE IN *CRUZADOS*
FROM 1580 TO 1584	189,770 (YEARLY AVERAGE)
1605	180,000
1606	?
1607	66,000
1608	50,000
1609	176,030
1610	?
1611	100,000
1612	120,000
1613	?
1614	90,000
1615	172,500
1616	40,000
1617	201,000
1618	120,000
1619	80,000
1620	80,000
1621	80,000
1622	142,000
1623	109,000
1624	109,000
1625	80,000
1626	110,000

TABLE 2
Quantity of *reales* sent from Lisbon and arriving at Goa and Cochin for the purchase of pepper.

In the same document, the exported monetary specie is clearly designated as 8 *reales* and 4 *reales* but excludes the 2 *reales* and 1 *real (singelos)* for they were not well accepted in the eastern market and were thus forbidden in the King's consignment.

Where did such a large quantity of Spanish minted silver come from? After the dynastic union between Portugal and Spain, silver arrived in Lisbon via two routes, either via Seville or more or less illegally smuggled.

We know from another document dated 1615 that in the same year the *"Casa da Índia"* obtained a license, thanks to a royal authorization to receive the amount of 200,000 *cruzados* in 8 *reales* and 4 *reales* to buy Indian pepper. This license was then renewed in 1616 and most probably also during the following years *(Trigueiros, 2009, no prelo)*. Much later, it was the Portuguese *"Casa da Índia"* itself that ordered a supply of American silver minted in 8 *reales* and 4 *reales* on its own account to be transported via Seville and later shipped in the naus leaving for the sea-route to India, according to a document relating to the year 1623.

However, it was not only after having disembarked in Seville that Mexican and Peruvian silver found its way to Portugal. Quite frequently the shipments were deviated well before they reached the destination port, either at the compulsory stop in the Azores, or because storms and pirates forced the galleons to look for refuge in metropolitan Portugal ports. It is calculated that in 70% of the cases, vessels that did not unload their cargoes of precious metals in Seville, did so in Lisbon.

Historical records are particularly clear on this subject: in Portugal silver was in shortage and it was paid for at a higher price than in Spain. All the *reales* coming from Seville or from Spanish galleons that entered left again destined for Goa, Cochin, Malacca and Macau.

Let's recall one particular case, relating to the year 1609: Portuguese *naus* unloaded 32 boxes of wood with *reales* in Goa that year. They were meant for the purchase of pepper and were later transported to Cochin the same way that they had arrived, that is to say, closed, tied up and marked. Inside were bags of coins, made of simple straw. When the Royal opened the bags, he noticed that they contained large quantities of 1 *real* coins instead of 4 *reales* and 8 *reales* coins, an illegal abnormality which infringed upon the established rules *(Godinho, 1981- 1983b)*. Consequently, in 1612 strict measures were taken in Lisbon to avoid the mixing of coins in the king's consignments so that 1 *real* coins and 2 *reales* coins would not be added to the cargoes of 4 *reales* and 8 *reales* coins, which were better accepted in the East Indian market.

Returning to our question about the possible sizes of the money chests, and based on the money values received in Goa referred to in the above table and the document cited we could see that in the year 1609 a total of 176,030 *cruzados* (equivalent to 1,564,711 *reales*) were transported in 32 wooden boxes. The logical calculation would be dividing the total amount of *cruzados* between the number of boxes and that amounts to 5,500 *cruzados* per box or crate (equivalent to *48,897 reales*).

Then, how many straw bags with money were transported in each crate?

During the excavation of the *São José* wreck site, a total of 65 artefacts were recovered. 31 of them were clumps of silver coins and 28 of them were groups of loose coins. The clumps of coins consisted mainly of silver coins and cannon balls. Other clumps consisted only of coins and in 6 cases they still preserved the original shape of their container which seemed to be a small bag where approximately 1,000 coins were packed *(Fig.37)*.

These "bags" of coins were very compact and no trace of the soft material used to avoid scratching during transportation, was found. Only one of these "bags" seemed to be fairly complete, where only a few coins, if any were lost. This was artefact number 2095, containing a total of 789 coins with a value of 4,796 reales in a mixture of approximately 60%-40% of 8 and 4 *reales* coins. Hence it can be concluded that each "bag" was packed with a value of approximately 5,000 *reales* at the departure point, but this is only an assumption. *(Fig.38)*

FIG.37
Coin cluster No. 2111 still in the shape of the straw bag.

FIG.38
The most complete coin cluster (No. 2095) from the wreck. It contained the equivalent amount to 4,796 reales.

As a result of this analysis we could conclude that the money in the Portuguese *naus* of the early 17th century was transported in boxes of approximately 5,500 *cruzados (48,897 reales)* containing 10 bags of ap- proximately 550 *cruzados* each *(4,889 reales)*.

But then an inevitable question arises: How heavy these boxes were? Were they manageable?

A silver coin of 8 *reales* weights around 25-27 gr. (equivalent to 3.125-3.375 gr. per 1 *real*), so we can take an average of 3.2 gr. weight per 1 silver *real*. Based on the above calculation, each box containing 48,897 *reales* would have to have weighed approximately 156 kg just in its silver content. To this we have to add the weight of the box itself, which must have been strong enough to hold such a weight in silver and that would take us up to approximately 180 kg per box.

We are aware that heavier objects than that, such as cannons and anchors, were commonly carried on these ships, but chests of money were supposed to be easily handled. Countless are the archival reports of Portuguese castaways who saved the King's money after a wreckage by moving the crates to the shore in a fairly short space of time and under extremely adverse weather conditions. Upon arrival at shore, they often traveled very long distances carrying the chests of money to the safety of a Portuguese settlement. Therefore the weight of 180 kg per box (that would demand 4 to 5 people to carry it) seems quite unlikely to us.

Moreover, in the particular case of the *São José*, the archival documents refer that they lost 9 chests of silver containing 18,000 cruzados of the King's money in the wreckage. That would lead us to believe that each chest contained 2,000 *cruzados* (17,777 *reales*) on average, leaving the figure of 5,500 *cruzados* per box very far out.

So let's go back to the archaeological evidence gathered during the excavation of the *São José* and calculate again. The total amount of silver coins recovered from that wreck site was **23,211**. The proportion in the denominations on the numismatic sample (**7,525** numismatic coins) showed a pattern of approximately 60-40 relation between 8 *reales* and 4 *reales* coins. Assuming that this proportion of denominations does not change in the remaining recovered coins (eroded coins + washers), we can calculate that from the overall amount of recovered coins (23,211) 13,541 were of 8 *reales*, 9,623 of 4 *reales* and 49 of 2 *reales*, amounting to an overall value of **146,918** *reales* recovered from the wreck.

Knowing that in the early 17th century the value of the Spanish *"peso de a ocho"* (piece of eight or 8 *reales*) was approximately 0.9 *cruzados*, we can calculate that the overall value in *reales* recovered from the wreck represents the value of **16,528 cruzados**, leaving only **1,472 cruzados** from the reported King's money lost which is around **8%** of the total amount. Taking into account the natural degradation of the silver immersed in seawater for 385 years, the mechanical action of waves and surge and the complete coverage of the site by sand, we can consider that recovering **92%** of the lost coins comes as fairly strong evidence that the reported amount of money lost was accurate *(Mirabal, 2007)*.

Bearing in mind this evidence, using as example artefact number 2095 mentioned above and assuming that all of the bags inside each crate were similar (in fact, each bag must have contained the same value; it was the value of the filled bag that counted and not the quantity of coins, a practice still followed today by some mint houses) the calculation couldn't be easier.

Each box in the *São José* must have been carrying approximately 2,200 *cruzados* (20,000 *reales*), stored in 4 bags of 550 *cruzados* each (5,000 *reales*), with a silver weight of 64 kg and a total weight of approximately 75 kg. This option seems more feasible to us than the previous one.

This is an example of how the combination of historical sources and archaeological evidence can answer some of the long time questions.

Conclusions

With regards to monetary and numismatic history, one can now understand the importance of the marine archaeological recoveries performed on the shipwreck site of the *nau São José* (1622) along the coast of Mozambique.

The statistics of the recovered coins and their respective denominations present at the site thus complete and confirm this theory: a staggering majority of 8 *reales* coins (59%) and of 4 *reales* coins (41%), as well as a very low percentage of 2 *reales* coins were found. The conclusion is now obvious: in 1622 the strict control of specie which was being shipped to India was fully accepted and in place, as mentioned above.

Of these *reales*, it is now known that there were several bags on board the *São José* which contained coins of Mexican and Peruvian origin only, as well as other bags with mixed coins from the mint houses of metropolitan Spain and the Americas.

Lastly, the historical information recorded and studied by Professor Magalhães Godinho is also confirmed when analyzing the dates struck on the recovered coins along with the dates estimated for the coinage and the initials of assayers. For instance, the most recent dates on the coins minted in Mexico go from 1600 to 1621 and make up 97% of the total of Mexican coins in the cargo. The same thing occurs with the coins minted in Potosi, as a great majority of the Peruvian coins in the cargo date from 1600 to 1621.

FIG.39
Silver coins before conservation.

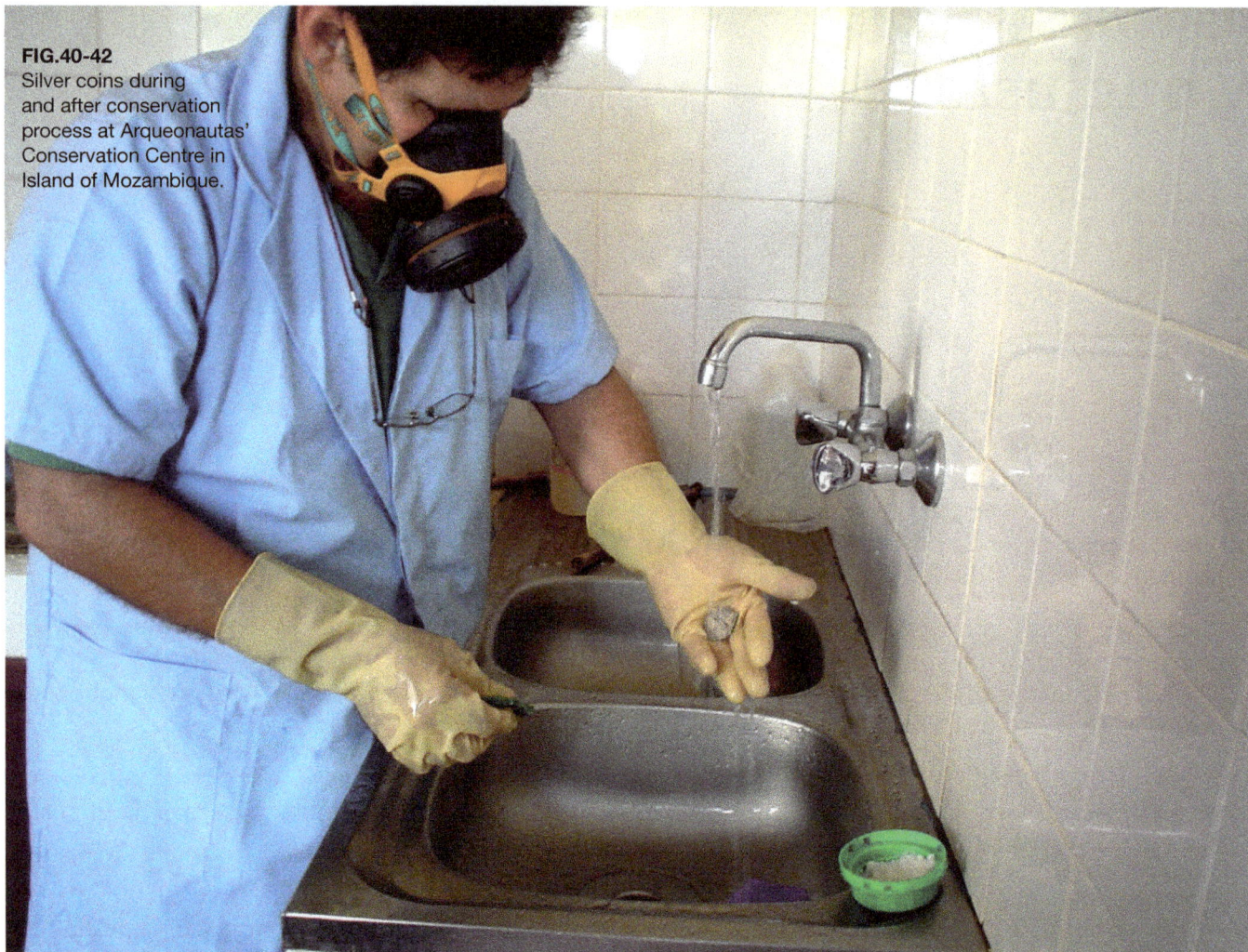

FIG.40-42
Silver coins during
and after conservation
process at Arqueonautas'
Conservation Centre in
Island of Mozambique.

FIG.41

MOG 003-05-2095

FIG.42

On the other hand, among the coins of metropolitan origin and minted in several cities of Spain, the date 1622 appears on the 8 *reales* coins minted in Seville. This is without doubt the most interesting specie from this recovery, apart from the other recent dates from the same origin, which make up 34% of the total analyzed.

Knowing that the *São José* left Lisbon on 22 March 1622 with a considerable cargo of silver coins in the form of *reales* on behalf of the king, the archaeological recovery operation allows historians to confirm that the bags which were shipped in Lisbon were originally from the *"Casa de Contratación"* in Seville. They had been packed together with Mexican-Peruvian coins, which had arrived in recent years, and with metropolitan Spanish coins minted recently, in order to make up the amount required to be transported to Lisbon and later to Goa.

This is to say that in 1622 the royal authorization referred to earlier with regards to the years 1615 and 1616 was still in place. All of the king's silver came from Seville.

In the selection studied, one can observe the numismatic aspects of the different mint houses which produced them, the master assayers who certified them, as well as the different minting techniques in use in the American mint houses, when compared to the metropolitan mint houses. Furthermore, and above all, one can observe the monetary, commercial and diplomatic history linked to these coins, from the end of the 16th and beginning of the 17th centuries, as referred to in the analysis above.

These are coins that can tell a whole story about what was happening along the coast of the Island of Mozambique, during an era in which silver *reales* from Castile were a merchandise of highly esteemed value in the spice trade between East and West.

This part of history is particularly well documented in the selected samples, which are now part of Mozambique's cultural heritage.

Bibliography and sources

ARCHIVAL SOURCES

AHU, India, Caixa 15, no 177, flo 5v

Archivo General de Indias. Indiferente, 1142. Carta de Tomás de Larraspuru, 31/10/1621.

BALL, Alexander, *(1622) Letter to the President of Batavia. [In the Fleet of Defence] October 20, pp. 132-210.*

Biblioteca Nacional de Lisboa; *Reservados; Caixa 26, no 153. Título da página de rosto: Armadas que partiram para a Índia (1509-1640).*

Biblioteca Nacional de Lisboa; *F.G. 1540; flo 127 / 128vo. Título: Relação do que passámos na viagem depois que passámos a linha e encontrámos os inimigos Ingleses e holandeses. "Itinerário do Padre Jerónimo Lobo".*

Biblioteca Nacional de Lisboa, Fondo General 1817.

Documentação Ultramarina Portuguesa, (1962) vol. 2, CEHU, pp. 503- 504.

PUBLISHED BIBLIOGRAPHY AND SOURCES

AAVV (1965), *Atlas*, Ed. Marcos Jiménez, In Cobb 1945 - *Relaciones Geográficas del Perú*, VOL. II, Madrid, pp. 126-35.

BARGALLÓ, Modesto. (1955) La minería y la metalurgia en la América española durante la época colonial. México, Fondo de Cultura Económica, p. 243.

BARRÓN, Amalia. (2000) *"Potosí, lágrimas de plata".* El Correo de la Unesco, marzo 2000. pp-3,4.

BOXER, Charles R. (1930) *"Dom Francisco da Gama, Conde da Vidigueira, a sua viagem para a Índia no ano de 1622. Combate na- val de Moçambique em 23-25 de Julho de 1622"*, Imprensa da Armada, Lisboa, p. 6.

COBB (1945-50 et ss). *Relaciones Geográficas del Perú*, II, 126-35 (Marcos Jiménez de la Espada. Introd. de José Urbano Martínez Carre- ras. BAE 184. Madrid: Atlas, 1965) All quotes from Potosí are taken from Gwendolin B. Cobb 1945 y 1949.

GODINHO, Vitorino Magalhães, (1981-1983b) *Os Descobrimentos e a Economia Mundial*, 4 vol. 2.a ed. Lisboa.

PELLICER i Bru, Josep. (1997) *Glosario de maestros de ceca y ensayadores (siglos XIII-XX)*. Madrid.

SELLSCHOPP, Ernesto. A. (1971) *Las acuñaciones de las cecas de Lima, La Plata y Potosí, 1568-1651*. Barcelona, Asociación Numismática Española.

VILAR, Pierre (1990) *O ouro e a Moeda na História*, trad. Portuguesa, Pub. Europa-América, Lisboa, p. 197.

NOT PUBLISHED BIBLIOGRAPHY AND SOURCES

DÍAZ GÁMEZ, Alfredo, (2008) Comentarios Numismáticos, doc.avulso, La Habana.

MIRABAL, Alejandro, (2006) Intermediate Report on Underwater Archaeological Excavations off the Island of Moçambique and Mogincual from April to November 2005, Moçambique, Janeiro de 2006.

MIRABAL, Alejandro, (2007) *Statistics and Considerations of the coins recovered in the MOG-003 wreck site by the end of 2006 season*, doc. avulso.

PROCTOR, Jorge A. (2006), Numismatist, Laguna Hills, California (USA), *personal communication.*

TEDESCO, Carol, (2008) Numismatist, Historic Research and Certifi- cation, Inc. Historic Underwater Discoveries, Inc. *Personal communication.*

TRIGUEIROS, Antonio, (2009) *Alguns comentários sobre as moedas recuperadas nas escavações arqueológicas do naufrágio da nau São José de 1622, ao largo da Ilha de Moçambique, doc. avulso, Lisbon.*

www.ingramcontent.com/pod-product-compliance
Lightning Source LLC
Chambersburg PA
CBHW052118020426

42335CB00021B/2816